SAM SHEPARD

Tooth of Crime

Sam Shepard is the Pulitzer Prize–winning author of more than forty-five plays. He was a finalist for the W. H. Smith Literary Award for his story collection *Great Dream of Heaven*, and he has also written the story collection *Cruising Paradise*, two collections of prose pieces, *Motel Chronicles* and *Hawk Moon*, and *Rolling Thunder Logbook*, a diary of Bob Dylan's 1975 Rolling Thunder Review tour. As an actor he has appeared in more than thirty films, including *Days of Heaven*, *Crimes of the Heart*, *Steel Magnolias*, *The Pelican Brief*, *Snow Falling on Cedars*, *All the Pretty Horses*, *Black Hawk Down*, and *The Notebook*. He received an Oscar nomination in 1984 for his performance in *The Right Stuff*. His screenplay for *Paris, Texas* won the Grand Jury Prize at the 1984 Cannes Film Festival, and he wrote and directed the film *Far North* in 1988 and cowrote and starred in Wim Wenders' *Don't Come Knocking* in 2005. Shepard's plays, eleven of which have won Obie Awards, include *The God of Hell*, *The Late Henry Moss*, *Simpatico*, *Curse of the Starving Class*, *True West*, *Fool for Love*, and *A Lie of the Mind*, which won a New York Drama Desk Award. A member of the American Academy of Arts and Letters, Shepard received the Gold Medal for Drama from the Academy in 1992, and in 1994 he was inducted into the Theatre Hall of Fame. He lives in New York.

ALSO BY SAM SHEPARD

Tooth of Crime

SAM SHEPARD

Tooth of Crime

(Second Dance)

A PLAY WITH MUSIC IN TWO ACTS

Music and Lyrics by T Bone Burnett

VINTAGE BOOKS

A Division of Random House, Inc.

New York

A VINTAGE ORIGINAL, FEBRUARY 2006

Copyright © 1974, 2006, copyright renewed 2002 by Sam Shepard

All rights reserved. Published in the United States by Vintage Books,
a division of Random House, Inc., New York, and in Canada
by Random House of Canada Limited, Toronto.

This is a revised edition of the work originally published as
The Tooth of Crime by Grove Press, New York, in 1974.

CAUTION: This play is fully protected, in whole, in part, or in any
form, under the copyright laws of the United States of America, the
British Empire including the Dominion of Canada, and all other
countries of the copyright union, and is subject to royalty. All rights,
including professional, amateur, motion picture, radio, television,
recitation, and public reading, are strictly reserved. All inquiries
for performance rights should be addressed to the author's agent,
Judy Boals, Judy Boals, Inc., 307 West 38th Street, #812,
New York, NY 10018.

Vintage and colophon are registered trademarks
of Random House, Inc.

Library of Congress Cataloging-in-Publication Data
Shepard, Sam 1943–
Tooth of crime : (second dance) : a play with music in two acts /
Sam Shepard ; with music and lyrics by T Bone Burnett.—Rev. ed.
p. cm.
I. Burnett, T Bone. II. Title.
PS3569.H394 T6 2006
812'.54—dc22
2005045661

Vintage ISBN-10: 0-307-27498-5
Vintage ISBN-13: 978-0-307-27498-4

Book design by Rebecca Aidlin

www.vintagebooks.com

Printed in the United States of America
10 9 8 7 6 5 4 3 2 1

Preface to the Revised Edition

Back in the sixties I was playing with the idea of a war of language—a duel where words were the actual weapons, the bullets. When I arrived in London in the early seventies, a largely unheralded play, *AC/DC* by Heathcote Williams, struck me as being an opening in that direction. Not only was the language uncanny but it also had the aura of assault about it. Bertolt Brecht's *In the Jungle of Cities* was another catalyst, but I wanted to make a totally American rendition and wound up somewhere between the old classic Western and rockstar nihilism. In 1972 (when the play was first performed at the Open Space in London) it seemed to me that rock and roll, as we had known it up till then, was being transformed into a river of sameness. It was beginning to lose its original fire and brass balls, much the same as American cars lost their verve in the transition from the fifties to the sixties. Long story short—the subject was "change," and I wanted to place each of these characters (Crow and Hoss) directly across the fence from each other. The original production was perceived as futuristic, verging on science fiction, but by 1996, twenty-four years later, it seemed dated to me and somewhat hackneyed. The DJ character felt like a cartoon. Hoss seemed needlessly melodramatic, and the language of Crow had lost its sting. So, again, I set about revamping the entire play through re-hearsals at the Lucille Lortel Theatre in New York. This process of rewriting a play while it's in rehearsal can be nerve-racking to actors and directors, and I'm sure the production suffered as a result, but in the end the play now is less simplistic and has a rhythmic flow that it lacked in its first rendition.

Sam Shepard
July 2005

Tooth of Crime

Tooth of Crime (Second Dance) was produced by Signature Theatre Company (James Houghton, Founding Artistic Director; Thomas C. Proehl, Managing Director; Elliot Fox, Associate Director) and Second Stage Theatre (Carole Rothman, Artistic Director; Suzanne Schwartz Davidson, Producing Director; Carol Fishman, Associate Producer) at the Lucille Lortel Theatre in New York City on December 15, 1996.

HOSS	Vincent D'Onofrio
BECKY	Rebecca Wisocky
MEERA	Sturgis Warner
RUIDO RAN	Jeffrey Anders Ware
CHASER	Jesse Lenat
DOC	Paul Butler
CROW	Kirk Acevedo
REF	Michael Deep

Directed by Bill Hart
Music and lyrics by T Bone Burnett
Set design by E. David Cosier
Costume design by Teresa Snider-Stein
Lighting design by Anne Militello
Sound design by David Van Tieghem
Video design by Kevin Cunningham
Musical direction by Loren Toolajian
Production stage managed by Ruth Kreshka
and James FitzSimmons
Casting direction by Jerry Beaver and Associates

The Tooth of Crime received its premiere at the Open Space, London, on July 17, 1972.

HOSS	Malcolm Storry
BECKY LOU	Petronella Ford
STAR-MAN	Michael Weller
GALACTIC JACK	Tony Milner
REFEREE/CHEYENNE	Tony Sibbalt
DOC	John Grillo
CROW	David Schofield

Directed by Charles Marowitz
Assistant directed by Walter Donohue
Set design by Robin Don
Music composed by Sam Shepard
Music arranged and played by Blunderpuss

Act I

Scene: A bare stage except for an evil-looking dark chair with a high back, something like an Egyptian pharaoh's throne but simple, center stage.

(HOSS *enters.*)

HOSS: *Song:* "Anything I Say Can and Will Be Used Against You"

ANYTHING I SAY CAN AND WILL BE USED AGAINST YOU

People tell me I look like hell
Well I am hell
I got a torture chamber orchestra
At the Delirium Hotel
I got an hallucination rattlesnake
To twist my skill through
You're my friend
But I'm gonna kill you

Somebody's got to monitor all this darkness darkness darkness
Somebody's got to locate the bomb dot com
Somebody's got to break out through the night so starless starless
    starless
Those who would overthrow the status quo

Soul like smoke hole in the sky
Gotta cry gotta cry gotta go gotta go gotta go
Target Arab chic MK ultra satellite blowup
Kill the pain let it rain let it rain

    I will disengage your mastery
    Until all you love is blasphemy
    Then I'll break in through your idiocy
    And twist your desire hideously
    And when you're the object of complete derision
    I'll make you a star on television
    Then if you want fame at a greater strength
    Speak to my girl Friday the thirteenth

Got no background
Got no files
Crawl through the cable black op ground zero no flight zone
All alone all alone all alone

    This is a story which is based on a true story
    Which is based on a lie

Don't jack with me Sahib
I'm history
Don't jack with me Lucille
I'm gone
I'm gone
I'm gone

(BECKY *enters.*)

BECKY: Choogin, Hoss. Choogin. The short is online. Wanna peek at the toys?

HOSS: Yeah, let's have a look. Jeweler check 'em out?

BECKY: Clean and blue. Gave his little stomp of approval. You know how he gits.

(BECKY *lays out the "weapons" on the floor: Strange-looking devices; weird mixture of swords, guitar necks, microphones, CBs, pistols, etc.*)

HOSS: Merc's set?

BECKY: Greased, lubed, and banging on all eight. Chaser slammed it up to 180 on the old Ventura Freeway. Said she didn't bark once.

HOSS: Yeah. About time he quit them quarter-mile bursts. That double-throat's gotta git time to blow out. Holley

9

made that carburetor back then for a reason. Old-time but it still hauls ass.

BECKY: No question there.

HOSS: Chaser fit?

BECKY: I don't gumbo with Chaser. You know that. He keeps to his own self.

HOSS: You watch him don't ya? Observe?

BECKY: I seen him chase his bacon around the plate with a fork this mornin. Asked him if that's where he copped his handle.

HOSS: So, how's he movin?

BECKY: Same.

HOSS: Did he look inclined to Boogie?

BECKY: He's always got the horns on for Road Rankin, you know that.

HOSS: Then we're good to go?

BECKY: I'd best check the Chart Man if I was you, Hoss. The Gazer.

HOSS: How's that.

BECKY: Just an inklin. A tickle. Won't hurt.

HOSS: We ironed all that through, didn't we? Week ago? I thought Meera gave me a green lane? I don't need hesitation now.

BECKY: Shit shifts, you know. Every two seconds somethin's slidin. He can't suss it all. Tell you the damn truth, some a them chart patterns he's honkin go back to the late fifties. Meera's antique in a lotta zones Hoss. I wouldn't bite the whole red apple he throws out, just cause it rolls.

HOSS: Git his ass down here!

BECKY: All righty. Don't sting my tail just for flaggin a dingo. I'm yer cold bitch, remember?

HOSS: Just buzz his booty! Now!

BECKY: Yabadaba Honk Man.

(BECKY *exits.*)

HOSS: (*alone*) Chingaflack! Tickles, inklings, cross-information! I'm good to go, here! Can't get stoved up by bad help and superstition. I need the points! Can't they see that? I'm winning in three fuckin states! Controlling more borders than any a them punk Markers. The El Camino Boys. Bunch a slump chumps. Threw down on that whole raggedy tribe back—back when? El Monte Legion Stadium? La Puente? What was it? Done deal. They were sliming. Where's the history here?

(MEERA *enters with* BECKY. *He carries his divining parapher-nalia—strange boxes and electronic projection devices that look all jerry-rigged and somewhat outdated—maybe even an old 45 record player.* MEERA *gets completely tangled up in the wires and plugs of his equipment.*)

HOSS: (*to* MEERA) All right, slick face, what's the skinny? Can we move now? Becky tells me you're hedging.

MEERA: Pretty dicey, Hoss.

HOSS: What! I knew it! I knew it! Week ago you give me green lights! Solid. No question. Now, it's no slice. What's the sudden shift?

MEERA: Patterns, Hoss. Meshes. I'm sussing every way I can to keep up but some of my equipment is just getting blown away by all these new waves. I can't even read some a these ciphers. Watch. I'll show you.

(MEERA *begins to set up his boxes, plugging them in, transferring wires, adjusting screens and keyboards, etc.*)

HOSS: I don't wanna hear this! If we needed new equipment, why wasn't I informed? I'd be glad to pay for new equipment. I thought we were up-to-date here.

BECKY: A new Gazer wouldn't hurt.

MEERA: I'm the best there is. Hoss knows that.

HOSS: I *don't* know that! I'm running on faith ninety percent of the time. Wing & a prayer!

MEERA: Just take a look at what I've got. That's all I'm asking. It's come down to techno-improvisation, Hoss. That's the only way to play it. All the data's bastard-info now. Vague vectors. Nothing pure. No essence source. It's all been scarfed and scarred to the bone. Take a look.

(MEERA *casts an image through his device.*)

HOSS: (*staring at image*) What's that?

MEERA: The El Caminos.

HOSS: I didn't bring you down here to look at pix of Roadkill! I'm ready for a Matar, man. A major Matar! I wanna move!

MEERA: You'll blow it.

HOSS: *I'll* blow it? What do you know. I've always moved on a sixth sense. I don't need your crossed-up, half-assed chart mix! We might as well be staring at box tops from Quaker Oatmeal. Might be more current than this shit.

BECKY: You gotta play privy to the Charts, Hoss. You never went against the Charts before.

HOSS: That was *before*. When Charts were Charts. Everyone was tuned to E Major back then. The Killing Floor was level. I'm falling behind now! Maybe you don't understand that! I'm falling behind because I'm still tuned to E Major!

MEERA: Not true, Hoss. No verdo. Lookit this. Take a look-see. (*He changes the image again.*) The El Caminos are about six points off the shuffle. Mojo Root Force is the only one even close enough to flutter and Mojo's got no turn of foot. Never had that bottom gear.

HOSS: Mojo? That Fruitcake? What'd he conk?

MEERA: Phoenix, Hoss. He slipped it while the Caminos threw camp, thinking he was outa range.

HOSS: Phoenix? That's my Mark! I claimed that ticket! He can't take Phoenix!

MEERA: It's done, Hoss. Least according to this jibe.

HOSS: That's against the Code! That's an out-and-out cry-down against the Code! Didn't the Keepers chop him?

BECKY: Keepers are getting usurped too, Hoss. Every-body's on the buyback.

HOSS: When did this shit happen? How come I'm the last to find out?

BECKY: We thought it'd rattle you too much.

HOSS: Rattle me! Nothing rattles me like knowing there's doo-dah going on behind my back!

MEERA: We weren't trying to keep it from you. Just tread-ing for the right timing.

HOSS: I'm gonna git that chump. I'm gonna have him clean. Mojo Root Force. He knew Phoenix was on my ticket! He's trying to shake me. That's it, is it? Thinks I'll jump borders and scam suburban shots.

MEERA: I wouldn't give him a whole lotta credit for strategy, Hoss.

HOSS: Well, I'm gonna crunch his bunker clean through. You watch.

BECKY: You can't bump against the Code, Hoss. Once a Marker strikes and sets up colors, that's his turf.

MEERA: Yeah, you can't strike claimed turf, Hoss. They'll pop you right outa the game.

HOSS: *He* did it! He took my mark! It was on my ticket!

MEERA: He'll just claim his wave system blew and he didn't suss it til it was too late.

HOSS: Well, he's gonna suss it now. I'll get a short fleet together and blow him out. He's gonna git so spun he'll think Phoenix is on the other side of the Antarctic.

BECKY: You gonna drop class? Is that it? Run with the Claimers? Sacrifice Solo Rights? You'll be a Gang Bopper again. A Punk Chump. Exile Bandito Trash. I ain't runnin with no Exile.

HOSS: I need the points! That Gold Record is not gonna wait for me to get straight with the Code. I'm not coppin to Ethical Suicide here, and miss a shot at a monster Matar. I need the fuckin points! I need a Kill!

MEERA: Best to hold steady, Hoss. This is a tender time. Lookee here. Just take a peep. Bits and choppers, but it scans.

(*He throws more images on walls, screens, set, etc.*)

HOSS: I don't need to visio more random road litter! I'm sittin on Ready!

MEERA: Just peek it. Timing. Wrong move'll set you back a year or more. Charts are moving too fast. Every day there's a new Star Marker now. You don't wanna be a Flyby. You want somethin durable, everlasting.

BECKY: He's choogin, Hoss. Loopy but choogin.

HOSS: He's dead meat. Look at this Vector shit on the wall! How do you make hide or hair outa this data mush?

MEERA: Patterns, Hoss. Matrix Mesh out there that needs new modes to conjure. I'm playing all this off the wall. Same as the rest.

HOSS: You're not comin up with an *action*! A *Kill*! You're fartin around in Info-Retard Land while my blood's on Go!

BECKY: Gotta listen to Management, Hoss. Fingering is everything.

HOSS: Management? This Zoombah can't even figure out the wiring anymore. Lookit him! Pathetic. Crawling through radio voltage from some lost World War his

Daddy can't remember. Git his ass gone! I need me a Forward Man. Git me a Dee Jay or something. One a the Stand Bys.

MEERA: A Dee Jay?

HOSS: (*to* MEERA) Git gone, Gazer. You've iced up in this crib.

BECKY: You're not firing him?

HOSS: (*to* BECKY) *You're* the one told me he was buckled!

BECKY: Yeah, but you can't just shunt him out on the Lone PrayerEE. They'll dice him up for quick snacks.

MEERA: (*gathering up his equipment*) I'll pack it. I was day-dreaming a change of scenery anyhow. Stagnation never was my cup of meat.

HOSS: (*still sitting*) I forged all my early Marks on Ruthless Culls. Ruthless. I'm not going soft now. Gotta kick out all the scruples. Go against the Code. That's what they all used to do. The Big Guns: Little Richard, Jerry Lee, Duane Eddy, Gene Vincent. They all broke Codes.

BECKY: But they were playing Doo-Dah, Hoss. They weren't Matando. You're a Killer, man. You're in the Big Bang.

HOSS: So were they. Cold Killers. Jerry Lee was *called* "The Killer." He even called himself that. Ask Meera. Go ahead, ask him. Ain't that verdo Meera?

MEERA: (*searching for a piece of equipment*) What? Have you seen my loodo adapter? Little blue job. I'm lost without it.

HOSS: Pathetic.

BECKY: You're rompin treason against the Game, Hoss. You could get the Carcel for less than that.

HOSS: Treason, shit. I know my power. I can go on Gypsy Kill and still gain status. There's a whole underground swell going on. Lots a Gypsy Markers comin up. Ain't that right Meera?

BECKY: Why do you keep consulting him? You just gave him the ax.

HOSS: I'm not consulting! I'm firmin up.

MEERA: (*collecting his gear*) I tell you what, Glib Man. This is free. Just before I hit the two-lane. I got nothin to lose by giving you the straight shit now. Shit you probably already got crawling through your skin. Reason you're so damn itchy and hot to trot. Yer day is down booga. Yer day is already been stepped on.

Sam Shepard

HOSS: (*to* MEERA) I might just have your heels chained to a pickup and drag you to Tijuana my own self.

MEERA: That won't stop it comin. The Game's bustin up. Any wrench-head can see that. The Game's too small now. Can't contain true genius. Next genius is gonna be a Gypsy Killer. You sussed that down the middle. What you omit though, and for good dang reason, is the Mark itself. That, you left neatly clean outa the picture.

HOSS: (*to* BECKY) Get this dogmeat outa here!

MEERA: That Mark is you, booga. None other. It's already in the jam. Done business.

HOSS: (*to* BECKY) I want a Dee Jay in here! One a the big ones! No standby. An original. Kidnap him if you have to! Get him here.

(BECKY *goes to escort* MEERA *and his equipment offstage.*)

MEERA: It's been sweet, Hoss Man. A sweet run. Some dandy kills that I could trace my brand to. I can see me getting minced soon's I cross the moat. That's only natural. But it's gonna be a waltz in daisies compared to what you got comin.

HOSS: Get him gone!

(BECKY *escorts* MEERA *off.* HOSS *left alone.*)

HOSS: (*alone*) Not premonition! Don't get tagged in that
key. Not suspicion! Shadow mode. Bring it back. Bring
it home, Hoss. Murder. Just plain murder. Blood. It's
simple. Do the simple thing.

(HOSS *goes into Song: "Make the Metal Scream."*)

MAKE THE METAL SCREAM

I see telepresence
Placeless space
Birdcage on a loop baby
Total waste

I feel greed infection
Tears of steam
It's the Jesus channel baby
Make the metal scream

I see blowdown damage
Static kill
Mean square displacement baby
Just for a thrill
I got no protection
No regime

Come electrocute me baby
Make the metal scream

> *I've seen his face so many times*
> *I know him blind*
> *Not enough action*
> *Not enough satisfaction*
> *By the time I trace this shakedown*
> *I'll be redesigned*
> *No piracy*
> *No privacy*

I got all the angles
Impicture force
In deformation baby
Without remorse

I got no reflection
To redeem
Come and lacerate me baby
Make the metal scream
Make the metal scream
Make the metal scream

> (BECKY *enters with* RUIDO RAN, *the Dee Jay, who carries with him a whole different collection of ramshackle electronic divining equipment.*)

BECKY: Snagged Ruido, man. Straight off the ruffle. Didn't have my patch out there two seconds and bam, he comes in loud and clear.

HOSS: Ruido Ran and the Radio Jam!

RUIDO: That's him, Slim. Heavy duty and on the whim. Backslappin sidetrackin, finger-poppin, reelin-rockin with the hot tips on the picks in the great Matando!

HOSS: You don't still have a show, do you? I mean, is there such a thing as "On the Air" anymore?

RUIDO: You jackin my flaps, Pony Man. Ruido Ran never *left* the Air. Ruido never touched down.

HOSS: Yer not still playing shit like "Wipe Out" and "It's a Lover's Question," are you?

RUIDO: Clyde McPhatter gained Sainthood, booga. Did you drop that one? Johnny Ace? Immaculate. Unworldly. Jackie Wilson. Heaven-born! Rufus Thomas—

HOSS: All right, all right. Just give it to me straight. Am I risin or fallin?

RUIDO: A shootin star niño. High flyin and no denyin. You is off to number nine!

HOSS: Show me what you got. Show it to me clean. Last Fool I had in here threw a lotta dung on the wall and hoped some of it might stick.

RUIDO: I can suss it. True Professionals are getting scarce and scary, these days.

HOSS: How's your equipment? Up to scratch?

(RUIDO *sets up his gear and begins throwing images up on the walls.*)

RUIDO: (*as he works*) State a dee Arc, Slim. State a dee Arc.

HOSS: I don't expect predictions or nothing. No Omen Sign. I don't need that. Just the straight scam.

RUIDO: I'm a Dee Jay, man. Born and bred. Diviner's not my game.

HOSS: All I'm lookin for is the natural landscape.

BECKY: Bebidas, boys?

HOSS: Yeah, bring us somethin red.

BECKY: This should be some slick shit.

(BECKY *exits.* RUIDO *keeps casting images on the walls, overlapping, as* HOSS *watches.*)

RUIDO: Okeedokey, here's the Stand on the National Band. Figment this. Game's clean for now. Solo is the word. Gang War is takin a backseat to the Honcho Singles. Low Riders are way outa the diamond and You is in, Slim. In like a stone Mata-Man.

HOSS: Don't stroke me, Ruido! I can exile your fanny just like the Meera. I want it straight. Just show me how it's movin.

RUIDO: Easy, Pony Man.

HOSS: I was game to take Phoenix clean and that meathead Mojo Root Force jumped it on me.

RUIDO: Yeah. I savvied that. Supposed to be on your ticket too. Crude swipe.

HOSS: He can't get away with that, can he? They got to chop him.

RUIDO: I can't dope them sheets, Hoss. You'll have to consult a Ref for the Rulebook or appeal to the Keepers.

HOSS: Appeal! I'm not appealing! Besides, I can't go to the Game Keepers. They'll demand an itinerary and question past Kills. I can't afford a penalty now! I need every point I've got!

RUIDO: Well, lookee here now. Gander this. There's action all around but no Numero Uno. No real Emergence. That's what they're backin their chips on you for, boy. The Bookies got you five to two.

HOSS: That close?

RUIDO: Gaze up there. There it is. Five to Two. Black and white. All of 'em runnin it down to you.

HOSS: No stretch run? Nobody on the rail?

RUIDO: Sprinters, man. Sprinters. You left the pack. I mean there's shys like Little Willard.

HOSS: East Coast?

RUIDO: Yeah.

HOSS: Willard's Solo now?

RUIDO: Stainless Steel, through and through, but no threat.

HOSS: How's that?

RUIDO: You really got some tailwind goin here.

HOSS: Just give it to me! Why's he out?

RUIDO: No breeze. Can't go the distance. Never even been around two turns yet.

HOSS: (*looks at image*) Who's that? That one there.

RUIDO: Studie Wilcock. Driving a beat-to-shit Vette with modified Chrysler cams. He ain't even on the dance floor.

HOSS: (*another image*) What about him? Who's that Mark?

RUIDO: Jade Monk. Supercharged Hudson Hornet. Slammed some corners and tried a hit on St. Paul. That's not your parish. Blew a head gasket tryin to cross the St. Croix. Rumor had him offed by the El Caminos. Probly better gone.

HOSS: The El Caminos? Those Chitos are pressin it pretty hard. They're gonna get the throw-down sooner or later.

RUIDO: No doubt. No need to pout. Course is clear. Maybe a handful of Gypsy Killers comin into the picture but nothing to fret your set.

(*Pause.*)

HOSS: What do you mean?

RUIDO: Lowrung. You know. Gypsy Matar. They rattle some caps then vanish. They been poppin in and out for some good while now.

HOSS: Gypsies?

RUIDO: Yeah, Dog.

HOSS: I knew it! Meera was right.

RUIDO: Meera?

HOSS: My Gazer!

RUIDO: The one you jogged?

HOSS: Yeah. He sussed it! He laid it out.

RUIDO: No, Hoss, look—They've drawn some side bets, that's all. They go anonymous cause of the Code. One slip and they is poked out clean. Snapped right off the map. Keepers won't even conk 'em.

HOSS: No! They've got a following. They're growing in the polls. I can sense it. The Hovays are flockin to Gypsy Kills.

RUIDO: Polls don't even tote their Kills for fear of the Keepers comin down on 'em.

HOSS: There's one out there! I can feel him. I know he's there. Meera nailed him cold.

RUIDO: You just got the buggered blues, man. You been whippin to the wrong pix. That Gazer got you stone scrambled.

HOSS: He's the only one who caught it and I fired him for it. (*calls off*) Becky! Becky Lou! I gotta get him back here before he gits across the moat. Becky!

RUIDO: You need to git a headset. Put yer ears on straight. These Gypsies is committin suicide. *We* got the Power. If the Keepers whimsy it, all they do is scratch 'em out. Simple. They're defeatee, man.

HOSS: They're comin. They're gonna turn the whole Game around on us. You watch. They *are* comin.

(BECKY *enters with drinks.*)

BECKY: Yaba, Honk Man.

HOSS: Where's Meera?

BECKY: The Gazer Loop?

HOSS: Yeah. Git him back here. I need to sit him down.

BECKY: We cut him clean loose, Hoss. Your whimsy, remember?

HOSS: Yeah, I remember! Now I want him back! I need to study up on one of his auguries.

BECKY: He has way departed, Hoss. I mean—gone.

HOSS: Track him! Git him back to me, now!

BECKY: Kelpies took his head off. Severed. Me and Chaser climbed the wall to watch. Nasty pack slaughter.

HOSS: Chingaflack!

BECKY: I thought you said, shunt him out. That's what we did.

HOSS: Gimme that!

(*He grabs both drinks from* BECKY, *drains them both, then smashes the glasses against the back wall.* RUIDO *is starting to pack up his gear in earnest.*)

RUIDO: I'm gonna shoobeedoo here, Hoss. I suss my function is on down the Pike.

HOSS: Not yet! I need some hint on this Gypsy Monger. Some clue.

RUIDO: I can't amigo there. I'm just a Doo Wop Dee Jay, Hoss. Old Shuffle. Future's not my forte.

HOSS: Chinga Future! I'm talking Now! He's out there! I can feel him. Real as Blacktop. He's chalkin me! Right now. Throw me some pix up on that wall.

RUIDO: I got no channel. Nothin to send or receive on. All I got is a lot a stacked up Info-Data.

HOSS: Why is there this sudden breakdown in the information department!

BECKY: There's nothing out there, Hoss. Nothin to come near to touchin your class.

RUIDO: Solamente uno.

HOSS: What do you know! We're all so damn insulated here. Watching Kelpie kills from high walls. Damn, why'd I turn that Gazer loose! He was my main line!

BECKY: Tighten down now. Quit jumpin at shadows. You need to take a shuffle cruise or somethin.

RUIDO: Now, there's a notion.

(*Pause.*)

HOSS: Yeah. Yeah, maybe that's it. Just some scouting. I'm feeling squashed up in here. Chaser ready to roll?

BECKY: Always.

HOSS: Maybe that's just the ticket. Shake these Banshees off. No action. Just a little cruise. I need to lay back— put my feet up on the dashboard.

BECKY: There ya go.

RUIDO: Shuffle off to Buffalo.

HOSS: That Gazer was half rambic anyhow. Every day he'd sift down a notch.

BECKY: You got that right.

HOSS: Didn't it seem that way to you?

BECKY: Absoloo.

HOSS: Every day he'd get to spinnin some weird Shinola. Probably had some inside hand with the El Caminos.

BECKY: No doubt.

HOSS: Spy Tout. Bet yer booty. Scumraker. Wish I'd sat on
that wall with you. Took his head clean off, huh?

BECKY: At the collar.

(CHASER *enters and stops.*)

HOSS: Chaser.

CHASER: Boss.

HOSS: Musta heard us ticking. How 'bout we take us a little
Cruise Shuffle. Merc's all open throat?

CHASER: I'd scotch that up for now, Hoss.

HOSS: Why's that?

CHASER: We just got word that Eyes sussed, somebody
marked you.

(*Pause.*)

HOSS: What? Marked *me*? Who?

CHASER: One a the Gypsy Trash.

RUIDO: I'm adios, Hoss. It's been jammin. Somehow, I got me a deep yearnin for the Old Radio Days, now. Tennessee Ernio. I suppose it'll pass. It's been jammin.

(RUIDO *exits. Pause.*)

HOSS: (*to* CHASER) A *Gypsy's* marked me?

CHASER: That's the word from Eyes.

HOSS: Where is he? This Gypsy.

CHASER: Phoenix, from what we know.

HOSS: Phoenix?

CHASER: That's what the Screen showed.

HOSS: Mojo! That must be it. He's hired a Gypsy to off me clean.

CHASER: Nope, he's Solo. We checked that through the horn. Total Renegade Solo.

BECKY: Horn's not the final note. Could easy be the Root-Force slipstreamin his time. Takin Hoss's marks and hirin dabblers to rub him out. It's a gang shot.

HOSS: Git Little Willard! Git ahold a Little Willard.

BECKY: Now don't fly off, Hoss. You're safe here.

HOSS: Safe! Safe and amputated from the neck down! I'm a Marker, not a cuff snapper! Get me Little Willard on the high line. Shake it! He'll remember the true-born days. We'll partner up.

(BECKY *exits.* HOSS *alone with* CHASER.)

HOSS: Now the tube tightens. I can stake it up. Draw to the straight outside or in.

CHASER: Cuidado, man.

HOSS: Phoenix is mine! It belongs in my back pocket. The West is mine. I'll just go and take on the Keepers. How's that? Live outside the Code altogether. Outside the whole shot.

CHASER: That's Gypsy scam. You're a King Marker, knockin at the top.

HOSS: Top a what? Nobody's playin by the Code no more. We been suckers to the Code for too long now. I say we get Little Willard, put a short fleet together. Then we roll right through this Gypsy and on to Phoenix. Mojo won't even know what hit him.

CHASER: Phoenix is sealed tighter than the paper on the wall.

HOSS: We rolled Bakersfield didn't we? That was tight.

CHASER: Tight but not sealed.

HOSS: We scorched Stockton.

CHASER: Yep.

HOSS: San Berdoo?

CHASER: Verdo.

HOSS: So Phoenix ain't iron ball.

CHASER: So it's back to the rumble?

HOSS: Don't get dramatic. It's temporary. Just temporary til we shake this Gypsy flash.

CHASER: I wouldn't riff it so light, Hoss. Some a these boys have built tough hide out there, circling the wagons all this time.

HOSS: What do you know about 'em? You heard some drift on these Gypsy dogs?

CHASER: They been lurking. Shinin the walls. I catch 'em out the mirrors sometimes, on surveillance cruise. Sneering like they mean something.

HOSS: How did Meera know? How do you figure?

CHASER: Just tuned to the cycle I guess. Elsewise he was taking a wild stab and hit home.

HOSS: Chaser, we were Warriors once. What happened? We ain't Markers no more. We ain't even Rockers. Just punk chumps, cowering under the Keepers and the Refs. We ain't flying in the eye of contempt! We've become soft, chewable, expendable muck lickers. What happened to our Killer heart?

CHASER: Still pumpin, Hoss. Still pumpin.

HOSS: For what?

CHASER: A taste a that gold.

HOSS: So yer backin down then? Backin down for a wall token. A tin badge?

CHASER: I'm just playing the Game, Hoss. I'm playing this one right here til a new one comes along. Now we best tighten up for this renegade. You don't wanna be sittin here in La-La when he comes knockin.

(CHASER *exits.*)

HOSS: (*alone*) Solo. Solo ain't the word for it. It's gettin lonely as an ocean in here. Little Willard's my last chance. Him and me. He's runnin without a driver, so can I. The two of us. Just the two of us. That'd work. That's enough against the Root Force. Fox this Gypsy altogether and head for Phoenix. (*Pause.*) You're not runnin, just strategizing. You're not running! You're not turning tail!

(BECKY *enters.* HOSS *jumps.*)

HOSS: You get Willard?

BECKY: No hook, Hoss.

HOSS: What! I told you to snag him! I need him now, bad!

BECKY: Blew himself away.

HOSS: No!! Willard? He was on the verge. He was choogin, just like me. He was in the top ten and rising!

BECKY: Found him slumped over an intersection somewhere in New Haven. Radio was still runnin.

HOSS: Why'd he wanna go and do a thing like that?

BECKY: Couldn't handle the bounce, I guess.

HOSS: Becky, I'm Marked! What am I gonna do? I was countin on Willard to make a move. The two of us. I can't just sit here and wait for this Gypsy to come tap on my hickory. What am I gonna do now?

BECKY: Sit him out. Least you'll know he's coming. You go out cruisin he's liable to strike outa nowhere. A Gypsy's got the jump on you that way.

HOSS: You think he'll take me, don't you?

BECKY: Not if you pull down, remember where you come from. He's got you shattered now. Cross–jumpin fragments. He's got some faraway touch on you already.

HOSS: What if I busted into Phoenix myself? Solo. Mojo'd never expect something like that.

BECKY: Mojo's not the Mark, Hoss. *You're* the Mark. And you best look dead in the eye of where it's comin from. If you don't take a good hard looksee, I believe you just might die a blind man.

HOSS: Wait him out? Sit and wait?

BECKY: Wait with a vengeance. Meet him on a singles match and bounce him hard.

HOSS: What if he snipes me?

BECKY: We got the watch out.

HOSS: I can't believe this! Backed into a cold box by an outside mongrel. Things have jumped that much. No apprenticeship! They just mark for the Big One. No sense of tradition whatsoever! Can't they see where this is going? Without a Code it's just Crime. Just plain old time Crime. No Art involved! No finesse.

BECKY: You want a shot or somethin?

HOSS: Yeah, git the Doc in here. (*She starts to go.*) Hey, Becky Lou— (*She stops.*) A singles match?

BECKY: Yeah.

HOSS: What mode?

BECKY: Mind Trains. What else? That's what he's cruisin for.

HOSS: Mind Trains?

BECKY: You're the one crying for Art and Finesse. Here's your shot. It's tailor-made.

HOSS: What if he picks weapons?

BECKY: It's your turf. Your call.

HOSS: Yeah.

(*Pause.*)

BECKY: You want the full load from Doc or cut some?

HOSS: Full.

BECKY: Be back. (*She starts to go again.*)

HOSS: Becky Lou?

BECKY: (*stops*) What?

(*Pause.*)

HOSS: I don't know. I just had this drop, like—like something moved away from me. Some—part of me.

BECKY: You want me to stay?

HOSS: Yeah. Just for now. I don't know what it was.

BECKY: It's just another Mark, Hoss. Take away the ribbon, it's just another Mark.

HOSS: Yeah.

BECKY: You'll find the pocket. Soon as he sallies in, you'll know.

HOSS: I never had this kind of doubt dose before. This— straddle. I've got no clue, Becky. Not a whiff. It's like he's comin from another planet or something.

BECKY: He might well be.

HOSS: Meera foretold it! He foretold it bane, Becky. Am I gone already? Is that it? Am I just like a buck in the crosshairs? Grazing? Ears pricked. Long gone before the powder even gets struck by the hammer? Is that what this is? Am I going through a pantomime ghost dance? Did Meera sound you something about the outcome?

BECKY: Nothing, Hoss. Nothin. Meera got his head took off. Right now, it's on display in Anaheim. Little glass case. I hear they're even scalpin tickets for it.

HOSS: Vanished. Took my secret with him. Easy to vanish.

BECKY: Yeah. Hard part is staying right here.

(BECKY *exits.* HOSS *alone. He begins to move around the space and talk to an imaginary Gypsy rival. He picks up some of the "weapons" from opening and tests them out.*)

HOSS: (*to himself and Gypsy image*) Choogin. Choogin, now. Secret's a secret. Unknown to me. Unknown to you. I'm *your* mystery. Figure *me*. Same. Figure *me*. Run *me* down to your experience. Chase this. An inch. Inch'll leave you fatal. Just an inch. Same. Mis-shift'll leave you murdered. Ha! Not that one, Shuga Man. Not that lunge. Shake this! (*He stops short, freezes. Pause, he listens, nothing.*) Vanished. No voice. No word. Gone. Just—gone. The Game. Keepers. Rock and Roll. Gone. All gone.

(DOC *enters with dope.* BECKY *behind.*)

DOC: You need a load, Hoss?

HOSS: (*in a daze*) Meera had his head took off. You hear that, Doc? His whole head.

DOC: Yeah. Well, might not a been too far from his natural state.

HOSS: Sometimes a snake'll go on living a little while like that. Broke in half. Two halves. Both still twitchin. I remember seeing my Daddy break a snake in half like that. Both ends twitchin.

BECKY: Hoss, you need something. You need to loosen down. A little prep-time. That Gypsy's bookin our way. You gotta wrap up & git fit, here.

HOSS: Need something. That's always been the case.

BECKY: Let Doc gaff you a little skin pop. Just to take the edge off.

(HOSS *rolls his sleeve up and* DOC *sets about shooting him up as* HOSS *continues to ramble.*)

HOSS: Broke clean in half. You're a doctor. How long can something live like that? Broke clean in half.

DOC: (*preparing syringe*) Depends. Snake's a different critter. Seen chickens run around half a day with no head. Just spitting blood out their necks and runnin in blind circles.

HOSS: Half a day.

BECKY: Meera never knew what hit him.

DOC: Turkeys. Ducks.

HOSS: Poultry must be tough.

DOC: Or stupid. One.

HOSS: How 'bout Gypsies?

(DOC *finds spot on* HOSS's *neck and matter-of-factly injects him there.*)

DOC: Never met one. Least not in this era.

HOSS: They had 'em in the Open Days?

DOC: Oh yeah, they had 'em. Remember one, name a Doc
   Carter. Mule Doctor I believe he was. Little got to be
   known as the man on account a the fact he was riding
   the shirttails of a certain William F. Cody. A pure pea-
   cock. All strut, no gut. Anyhow, this Doc Carter came to
   be known as "The Spirit Gun of the West," and a well-
   deserved title it was too. Man could shoot the hump
   offa buffalo on the backside of a nickel at a hundred
   paces. Cody used him as his dupe in all his Wild West
   Shows. Old Buffalo Bill would be out there pantomim-
   ing with blanks while Doc Carter sat tight behind a
   screen and plunked them silver nickels right outa thin
   air. Amazing spectacle, I was told. Old Doc never got
   out from behind the shadow a that Cody. I suppose
   nowadays he'd just take over the whole show, like I
   hear tell some a these Gypsies are.

HOSS: That's what you hear?

DOC: Rumors. Rumblings. You know.

HOSS: Whole System's gettin shot to shit, ain't it, Doc? The
   Code. Keepers. Markers. The whole fandango.

DOC: Well, I wouldn't go that far.

HOSS: These might be the very last days of honor. They might well be.

BECKY: Doc, haven't you got something to turn him around? He's been on this tailspin whim from sunup.

HOSS: There's no Cure for this. Ain't that right, Doc? No medicine to turn this squall around and force it back north. It's coming.

DOC: Well, there does seem to be some ripples in the air but I wouldn't put too much stock in a bunch of banditos runnin around shaking their tail feathers. You've got the history behind you. Experience. No replacement for that.

HOSS: It's all replaceable. Every inch.

BECKY: Hoss, you're knockin right at the top, hombre. Right at the top. Number one with a bullet. That gold's as good as in your palm. Now you gotta just knuckle down here and draw a line on this vandal. Zone in before he ever even gets to the moat.

HOSS: Maybe I need a little change a pace. Vacation or something.

BECKY: Vacation? Matando's full-time boogie Hoss. There's no vacation.

DOC: I heard about one little place. An island, where they don't play the Game. Everybody's on Downers all day long.

HOSS: That sounds choogin. What about that. Maybe you could line that up for me, Doc. All I need's a week or two. Just to gear down.

DOC: I'll see what I can do.

(DOC *exits*. HOSS *with* BECKY.)

HOSS: (*stoned, sings to himself*) "Take out the papers and the trash. Or you don't get no spendin cash." Who wrote that?

BECKY: Hoss? You trippin?

HOSS: (*sings to himself*) "Just tell your hoodlum friend outside. You ain't got time to take a ride."

BECKY: Don't backslide on me, Hoss. It's too late for that.

HOSS: (*stoned*) Cold white powder. Keep me from it. Pain free. Sweet white poison of the poppy. Beautiful flower. Don't let me see.

BECKY: Just cruise now, Hoss. Just coast.

HOSS: There's an inkling sneaking into me. Drip by drip.

BECKY: Just float, baby. Let it ride.

HOSS: A leak that's strong. Swelling at the seams. You feel it, Becky? It's aching to burst. Aching to come crushing through these walls.

BECKY: There's nothing, Hoss. Nothin you can't cop to. You've seen it all.

HOSS: I've seen everything but the thing I need to see.

BECKY: There's nothing new out there. Just trippin variations.

HOSS: No, not new. You're right. The same ancient demon dog. The same. Keeps chewing on us, silently.

BECKY: Tighten up, Hoss.

HOSS: Separated. Chewed the legs right off. We lost the simple thing.

BECKY: What'd Doc pop you with? You better reel it in, Hoss.

HOSS: The one on one. The tight connection. Lost it clean. (*sings softly*) "I'm walkin the floor over you." Ernest

Tubb. Blue sequins. Rollin. Just rollin. West Texas. One-night stands. Grand Ole Opry. Ryman Auditorium.

BECKY: Hoss! This Gypsy's comin here to chomp your liver and spit it out! Now what're you gonna do? Roll over like some fat old toothless dog and play dead? He's comin to eat your lunch, booga! Don't go yesterday on me.

HOSS: Daddy drove a thousand miles to see that show. A thousand miles. We sat around the radio like it was a campfire. Burnin through the night. Glowing. Red.

BECKY: Hoss! Git up! Git on your feet! Git your blood movin now!

HOSS: Blood. Now there's the thing. Blood. Unseen. Blue tube drained the blood away. Glowing blue. Blue now. Not red. Not bright. Cold blue. Like night. Sucked the blood right out. Removed us all. Phantoms flickering on the wall. Snuffed the campfires out. Sucked us empty into dreams of far-off victory. Plunged us shocked. The endless, bottomless image hole.

BECKY: Hoss, get up! Stand up now! You're fading.

HOSS: That's what it was. All that dreaming. Yearning. Hunger. Swapping today for tomorrow. Tomorrow's here and still not satisfied. Still not quite cracked up to be the crowning victory. Still hungry. Still devouring imagery.

BECKY: Hoss, it's bald out there. Gutted. Razed to the ground. Maybe you oughta take a little tour around the old neighborhood and get off the nod, just for kicks. Take a wee peek. Smokin. Grim and peeled to the backbone. It's a monkey now with no face, no body, and no name. And it's coming to git you, son. Sure as shimmy, it's comin to do you in.

HOSS: Cold white powder. Keep me from it. Sweet white poison. Beautiful flower. Don't let me see. Please, don't let me see.

(CHASER *enters.*)

CHASER: *Song:* "Kill Zone"

KILL ZONE

We stood together in the open field
And heard the secrets that the night revealed
Then we chased the lie
Racing through the sky

Can we untangle guilt or innocence
How hard we torture this ambivalence

Night will bring no dawn
Where has power gone

   For I'll steal your dreams while you are sleeping
   And sell them for dust and cheap lust
   And I'll slit your hope while you are weeping
   And wipe the blade clean with morphine
   Be my queen

The night prowls the dark clouds
That shroud the storm at sea
I'm dropping at too great a speed

   Come closer to me
   On your hands and knees
   Alone in the kill zone

How much is not enough how much is through
How long will I be getting over you
How much grief and sin
Til a heart caves in
Til a heart caves in
Til a heart caves in

   (DOC *enters.*)

DOC: Hoss, we got a visitor. We just got tapped, Gypsy's punched through Zone Five. He's approaching the Moat. Full bore.

HOSS: Good. That's good. What's his ride?

CHASER: You're not gonna believe this. '58 black Impala; fuel-injected, bored and stroked, full-blown underneath.

HOSS: My kind a outfit.

CHASER: Similar.

HOSS: Handle?

CHASER: Calls himself Crow.

HOSS: Crow. I'm gonna like this honcho. Let him on through.

CHASER: All the way?

HOSS: Yeah. Brake him at the Moat and sound him on a Mind Train Duel.

(DOC *exits.*)

CHASER: Mind Train?

HOSS: Something wrong with that?

CHASER: He didn't come all this way to fuck around in the argots. He's gonna want some blood.

HOSS: I know what he came for. I know exactly what he came for. Blood's too simple. No satisfaction. Cold slaughtered be just downright disappointing to both of us. Don't you think? Kind of a letdown in the face of what's at stake.

CHASER: I don't know. I always found it kinda thrilling, myself.

HOSS: Thrilling but short-lived. I wanna leave a brand on this Gypsy. One way or the other I'm gonna leave him branded.

CHASER: Mind Train. All right. I hope he bites.

HOSS: He'll bite. It's my turf. Right up to the drop, it's still my turf.

CHASER: I'll sound him.

(CHASER *exits.*)

HOSS: Becky Lou—You were right about the Mind Train. How'd you know?

BECKY: I seen it comin.

HOSS: Just like Meera.

BECKY: Yeah.

HOSS: I'm glad it's here. I'm glad it's finally here. I'm just dying to see his face.

BECKY: You best rest up, Hoss. It won't be long.

(BECKY *exits.* HOSS *alone.*)

HOSS: (*sings to himself*) "I'm walkin the floor over you. I can't sleep a wink, that is true." (*He stops and moves then stops again, as though listening for something. He sings again.*) "I'm hoping someday—that you'll come back to me." (*He stops and listens again then sings the last line.*) "I'm walkin the floor over you." (*He stops, listens.*)

END ACT ONE

Act II

Scene: The stage is the same.

   (CROW *enters.*)

CROW: *Song:* "The Rat Age"

THE RAT AGE

I was conceived in a behavior station
Light years from civilization
I was born in oblivion
Half Balinese half Libyan
My father was a vector
My mother was a spector
As Earthmen battle for their skins
I come down with the aliens

Is this not the rat age
The demented photostat age
The time of no room

Sam Shepard

Separate
We've broken the genetic code
And left it bleeding by the road
Where murderers loom

You've changed your face you've changed your scent
You've even changed your fingerprint
Image is anything

But with all this electricity
You can't change your publicity
The lies the many sing

    Down in the greedplex
    Under a spike of light
    Stop at the slave port
    Enter the death resort
    No stimulation
    Nothing but mono thought
    Resimulation
    Depop but don't get caught

    I dream to surf the rodeocean
    Negotiate meaning with no emotion
    If the kill is clean you still got time
    To hone evil on the tooth of crime

I'm sober on the grapes of wrath
While running down the psychopath

Is this not a cruel world
Good morning little schoolgirl
It's the rat age
The rat age
The rat age

> (CROW *moves about, thoroughly surveying the space, then finally flips himself onto* HOSS's *chair.* HOSS *enters. Pause.*)

HOSS: Sleuth tells me yer ridin a '58 Impala.

CROW: Razor, leathers. Very razor. Still in the style jam? Next we'll be reminiscing Bob's Big Boy, no doubt. Annette Funnycello.

HOSS: Old habits break hard.

CROW: You don't break 'em, you chop 'em off.

HOSS: I didn't invite you in here to get schooled, bug boy!

CROW: You didn't invite me, period. I'm yer Backdoor Man.

HOSS: Oh—So, Mr. Willie Dixon still remains on your list? You're not so far removed as I thought.

CROW: You can stretch yer imagination from here to the starry host and you won't come near to whiffin me, Mach Man.

(*Pause.*)

HOSS: Look—I didn't expect any generosity of spirit or anything. I know yer blood-game. Ruthless is a simple deal. A dumb deal. I've been wound tight to it since the days of the old Gas Wars. I just thought— (*pauses*)

CROW: Now that's yer breakdown right there, Leathers.

HOSS: What's that?

CROW: "Thought."

HOSS: All right—you want a bida? Something wet? Might as well kick this out.

CROW: (*laughs*) Couthie! Benign! Lush in sun time gotta smell of lettuce or turn of the century. Sure, Leathers, squeeze on the grapevine one time.

HOSS: White or red?

CROW: Keep it the color of the Killing Floor. Why create confusion?

HOSS: Don't drift. I'll be right back.

CROW: I'm where I'm supposed to be.

(HOSS *exits.* CROW *walks the space.*)

CROW: (*to himself, on the move*) Very razor. Gleaming. Polished. A sheen to the movement. Weighs out in the eighties from first to third. Keen on the left hand, although born on the right. Maybe forced his hand over. Butched some instinct down. Work it through the high range. Cut at the gait. Get past C. Middle C. The sweet simplicity. Cut at the gait. Heel toe rhymes of piano South. Deep blues bed. Can't suss that particular. That's well covered. Masked. Meshing patterns. Easy mistake here. Suss the bounce.

(CROW *tries to get inside* HOSS's *walk. Moving through space, experimenting.*)

CROW: (*continues moving*) Too heavy on the toe. Work the brazos down. Hold a mode. Here's one. Three/four cut time copped from Keith Moon. Early. Rare. Very spooky. Nihilistic era. Now. Where's that pattern. Slipped. Gotta be in the "Happy Jack" album. When the world was round. Records were round flat things. Grooves. There. Right around there. Triplets. Six/eight. Here it comes. Battery. Double bass talk. *Fresh Cream.* Ginger Baker. Where's that? Which track? Skip that. No. Skip. Skip. Yeah. Skip James! There it is! Skip James! Yeah. (*sings*) "I'm so glad, I'm so glad, I'm glad, I'm glad, I'm glad." Yeah. Ancient. Inborn. (*sings*) "Don't know what to do,

don't know what to do. I don't know what to do."
Terrible attachment. Terrible, terrible attachment. Gotta
be a surgery. Grind down.

(*He hears* HOSS *coming, darts back to the chair and sits.* HOSS
enters with wine.)

HOSS: Ya know I had an instinct you were coming this way.
I was on to a Gypsy pattern early yesterday. Even con-
jured going that way myself.

CROW: Cold, Leathers. Very icy.

HOSS: Yeah. It was a small lapse.

CROW: Backseat nights. Tuck and roll pillow time. You got
fur on the hide in this trunk.

HOSS: Yeah, yeah. No accounting for it. I'm just gettin
bored, I guess. I want out.

CROW: Out?

HOSS: Well—a changeup.

CROW: I pattern some conflict to that line. Animal says no.
Blood won't go the route. Redo me right or wrong?

HOSS: Could you—maybe back the language up a little.

CROW: Choose me an argot, Leathers. Singles, LPs, Lazer weave. Idiomatic mano. Radar band.

HOSS: I'm gettin a little gray to follow the flash, is all.

CROW: Solomon mist.

HOSS: I—I musta misfed my data somehow. I don't know. I thought you were gonna be raw, unschooled. Ya know? I mean maybe the training's changed since my time.

CROW: Very possible. Mighta been jumped altogether.

HOSS: Look—I wanna just sound you for a while before we get down to the cut. You think we could do that? You don't know how lonely it's been in this jam. I mean, I can talk to Chaser but we mostly wind up reminiscing on old kills. You know. Slip back into Bakersfield. Turf wars. I get no new information. Nothing's coming in. I'm starving for new food.

CROW: Spin me somethin.

HOSS: Now this don't mean I won't be game to mark you when the time comes. I don't sleep standing up. It's just that I wanna find out what's going on out there. None of us seems to have a clear picture, here. I mean all the pictures are—Nothing's making any sense. I'm surrounded by limbos still playing in the sixties. That's where I figured you were actually. Earlier in fact. Beach Boys maybe. Sad Brian Wilson.

CROW: That sand stayed on the shore with me, Leathers. Sure you can suss me in detail. What's your key?

HOSS: This is stark. Me bibing from you.

CROW: No guarantee.

HOSS: I mean I can't believe myself admitting it. A lack. You know? I thought I could teach *you* something. I thought you were maybe playin to the inside. Choosin me off just to get in the door. I mean I know you must be Mojo's trigger right? A throw-down artist?

CROW: Derail, Leathers. Yer smokin the track.

HOSS: Eyes traced a Phoenix route. It don't matter. If you ain't from the Root Force, your ass is grind. Any way you cut it yer a corpse. So let's lay that one on the rack for now. Let's just suspend and stretch it out.

CROW: We can breathe thick or thin. The air is your genius.

HOSS: Good. Now, first I wanna find out how the Gypsy Killers feature the Stars. Like me. How do I come off? Are we playin to a packed house like the Keepers all say?

CROW: (*cackles*) Those Image shots are blown off the hoodoo, man. No fuse to match the slot. Only trinsic power fields weight the points in our match.

HOSS: Well, we're not just being ignored! Somebody's payin attention out there. You can't tell me we haven't sent a few ripples your direction.

CROW: We catch debris beams from your set. Scope it to our action then scat it back to garbage game.

HOSS: Listen, chump, a lotta cats take this game serious! There's a lotta good Markers left in this league.

CROW: You choose ears against tongue, Leathers. Not me. I can switch to suit. You wanna patter on my screen for a while?

HOSS: It's just a little hard to take, is all. If it's true. I don't believe we could be that cut off. How could that happen? We're playing in a vacuum? All these years. All the kills and no one's watching?

CROW: Watching takes a side seat. Outside. The Game hammered the outside.

HOSS: And now you hammer us with fucking indifference! This is incredible! It's just like I thought. The Outside is the Inside, now.

CROW: Harrison Beatle did that ancient. It cuts a thinner slice with us. Roles fall to birth blood but we wing that by playing intergalactic modes. There's scores marked on Venus now, Leathers. Neptune, Mars.

HOSS: How do you get to Neptune in a '58 Impala!

CROW: How'd you get to earth in a flathead Merc?

HOSS: There! Right there! Why'd you slip just then? I sense a boggle. Some vague humanness. You're into a wider scope than I thought, bug boy, but there's a crack. You're playing my time Gypsy but it ain't gonna wash. And get the fuck outa my chair!

(CROW *slides out of the chair and cruises the space.* HOSS *sits in the chair, sips his wine. Slowly,* CROW *begins to assimilate* HOSS*'s walk until he's got it down perfect.*)

CROW: Yer tappets are knockin, Rock Man. I smell an internal smokin at the seams.

HOSS: I'm beginning to suss the mode, Crow Bait. Very deadly but no show. Time is still down to the Mark, kid, no matter what planet you visit. How's yer feel for Mind Trains?

CROW: More ancient pitter-patter? Smokey? Miracles? The Platters?

HOSS: Don't play mooncalf with me. Mind Trains is hiero-glyphic in any domain.

CROW: Breakdown lane. Side a the road days, Hoss.

HOSS: Yeah, well that's the way it's gonna be. Turf decrees the tenor. Even in your sphere.

CROW: Throwin to snake-eyes now, Leathers.

HOSS: (*voice shift*) So you gambled yer measly grubstake for a showdown with the Champ. Now ain't that a bit of pathetic. Pity and shame. Pity and shame. You young guns sproutin up outa prairie stock. Readin dime novels over breakfast. Drippin bacon fat down yer zipper. Pathetic. Gone blown right across the wide wasteland.

CROW: Cute shift, Leathers. Real cute. Time warps don't shift the purpose any more than bad acting. Yer clickin doorhandles now, hermano. There'll be more paint on your side than mine. Guaranteed.

HOSS: We'd drag you through the busted street fer a nickel. Naw, wouldn't even waste the gelding. Just crunch yer knees and leave ya fer dogmeat.

CROW: You're about tached out in second, aren't you Leathers? I'd go to overdrive right quick before the universal takes a shit.

HOSS: (*another voice shift*) You mugs expect to horn in on our district and not have to pay da price? Bosses don't sell out that cheap to small-time racketeers. You gotta toe the line, punk, or you'll end up just like Mibbsey.

CROW: Very nice slide, Leathers. Just when I had you pinned between second and third.

HOSS: Don't give me that! I had you gimpy. You were down on one knee! I saw you twitchin!

CROW: Sometimes the skin deceives. Shows a power ripple. Misconstrued, Leathers. Misconstrued.

HOSS: You were fishtailing all over the track! I had you tagged solid!

CROW: Posi-traction rear end. No pit stops the whole route. Maybe you got a warp in yer mirror.

HOSS: *You're* the warp in my mirror! You were dropped down!

CROW: Sounds like a bad condenser. Points and plugs maybe.

HOSS: Suck ass! I had you clean! And stop walkin like that! That's not the way you walk, that's the way *I* walk!

(*Sudden stop. They face off.* HOSS *rises slowly from chair.*)

HOSS: All right. All right, I can handle this. I'm seeing the face of this now. But I need a Ref. I ain't playin unless we score. Traditional. Blade to bone. Keepers rule.

CROW: It's yer party, Hoss. Scoring strokes you, let's score.

HOSS: I'm gonna take you Gypsy. I'm gonna whup you so bad you'll wish we had done the throw-down. Then I'm gonna send you back with a mark on yer forehead. A mark that won't never heal.

CROW: Yer crossin wires now, Leathers. My send is to lay you cold. I'll play flat out to the myth but the blood runs when the time comes. Sangre. Matar.

HOSS: Yer well padded, Crow Bait, but the layers'll peel like a skinned buck. I'm gonna get me a Ref now. You best use the time to work out. Woodshed a little. Get yer chops down. You need some sharpening up. When I get back it's head-to-head till one's dead.

(HOSS *exits.* CROW *alone, sings.*)

CROW: *Song:* "Mr. Lucky/Swizzle Stick"

MR. LUCKY/SWIZZLE STICK

Bongo rama llama Ram Das Kapital
Boo! Who are you know me

Sam Shepard

Bruja ya ya no no nah nah
Felon felon I can hear you coming even when you say good-bye
Jump through your skin sin sin has been Franklin

Revealing with the feeling in the eye is sci fi
In the back is black Jack no taste for sacrifice
I'll show you your desire if you think it
I can crack it through
I will give it to you
I will give it to you

> *I will turn your cool incendiary*
> *Then infiltrate your pride*
> *And lace your faith with cyanide*
> *Whatever fools the eye is true*
> *I will jerk the world from under you*
> *Swizzle stick*
> *Bleed! Distort!*

My constant aim is to spread sweetness and light
What's yours is mine kampf vanilla in Manila
Dig in Dig in Dig in sleek

In a rage in a cage
Call your marker darker darker

Church of Texas sky paint well born
Strategy of tension through the heart is high Art
In the neck is low-tech proper racial policy

The true source of light in a mirrored room
Doom Baby Doom

Through the brain feel no pain
In the throat no antidote

How do you spell?
Burns returns

> (*Song ends.* HOSS *enters with* REF, *dressed in traditional referee gear and carrying an odd collection of paraphernalia for scoring the "match."*)

HOSS: All right. All right, I hooked this one up off the old Corn Belt circuit. A little praxis but he'll work.

CROW: Whatever blows your skirt up, pony man. You know how tradition just twirls my ticket.

HOSS: I don't fancy tap dancers, Crow Bait. I like both feet nailed Joe Frazier–mode. He's gonna see to it that things stay clean. He's an absolute neutral Heartland Zombie. One of the best.

CROW: Scarce breed.

HOSS: Points scored and lost on deviation from the zero field state.

CROW: Well, I'd say you already broke the mercury in round one.

HOSS: There *was* no round one! That was a tune-up. We break when he's ready.

CROW: I can't cipher why you wanna play this course, Leathers. It's a far cry from street screech.

HOSS: Just to—show myself somethin.

CROW: Yerself? Yer own self? Yer self self?

HOSS: Yeah. I don't know how it is with you—but for me it's like looking down a long pipe. All the time figuring that to be the total picture. You lift your eye away for a second and see suddenly you been gypped.

CROW: "Gypped"? Coming down from "Gypsy" no doubt.

(*Pause.*)

HOSS: I'm gonna have fun skinnin you.

CROW: If narrow in the eyeball is your handicap then runnin a todos match figures perfect suicide.

HOSS: We'll see.

CROW: It took me all of thirty seconds to suss your gait. Ran it down to Skip James via Ginger Baker.

HOSS: I'm an open book.

CROW: Paranoid Skip James. Lowdown was he died a cancer of the balls from trying to hide his licks from all them white imitators. Like *you* for instance, maybe.

HOSS: I see you turnin me in. I'm stickin with this route, Gypsy. And that's exactly what you want so can the horseshit. There's no Marker on the planet can outgun me with any kind of weapon.

CROW: We're runnin Mind Trains, Hoss. Your choice.

HOSS: That's right! That's exactly right. Mind Trains.

CROW: Dig deep, booty. Put yer game face on. Yer about to feel the maniac.

(REF *blows his whistle and steps up.*)

REF: All right, all right. Let's get this show on the road. Now look, I want it clearly understood here—I myself, personally, have no particular ax to grind. I'm from Lincoln, Nebraska, and proud of it. Born, bred, and corn raised. At the age of eighteen I could break both you assholes in half with my bare hands. That's not a boast, that's a plain fact. Neither one of you's got the brains God gave a chicken, as far as I'm concerned. But I'm not in charge of the flow of time and if some distant motley mob out there figures the outcome of this little polka is worth a fart in the wind, then so be it. I'm just payin the rent. Now, I'm gonna score it like I see it and if there's any whining, bitching, or complaining of any kind, I'm walking back to Nebraska and you can kiss my white Midwestern ass. Are we clear on this? Have at it.

(REF *backs off. Music in.* HOSS *and* CROW *circle for the fight.*)

CROW: (*lurking menace*) At the get-go white face. Pale. Moon. Quiver. Blank sheet. Quiver. Shake from a wet wind. Shakin like a cold dog. Outside. Exile. Bone bare. Shun to the shiver. Barren. Shun to the moon moth. Poor dog. Quiver. Crackin from the outside. Crackin from the hide in. Hidden, hidden. Craving for belonging. Yearning for the fireside. Yearning for the warm touch. Yearning be your doomsday. Yearning for the front lawn. Barren, barren. Burned to the liver.

HOSS: Mock up, Crow Bait. Mock up. Circle. Wing it now. Show your oily purple feathers. Show me some wind jive now. Do your little doo-dah dance. Yer hoofin baby. You be hoofin now.

CROW: Kid's on his belly. Tits down on the tarmac. Belly to the blacktop. Slide through the parkin lot. Shame kid. Runt kid. Dumb with the losers. Side slash to the kid with the hitch walk. Slide. Shift. Slide kid. Whiplash. Dumb kid. Runt. The loser. The runt. American Hucklebuck. Muck it now. Muck it.

HOSS: Fishin, Crow. Fishin. No muscle to it.

CROW: No muscle needed. Hollow reed blow a tune right thru it.

HOSS: No sinew. No blood.

CROW: Human debris.

HOSS: You and me both hatched from the same dark mud.

CROW: But you never jumped it. Eyes still mired. Tongue bogged. Mushin with the weight. Dragged heavy. Down knee-deep in yer own shit.

HOSS: Better than borrowed.

CROW: Borrowed boogie. "Better" had its long sad day. Now it's done. "Better" bites it to the core. You still chaw on moral dick. "I like Ike and tricky Nixon" all that corpse chalk. Mired. Fucked in its own stew. Fucked in its sticky white peppermint pussy. Fucked in open empty Cold War puke dog. You take it up the ass and call yourself original. Dogs beat you to it. Monkeys. The double-backed huckin beast.

HOSS: Backsteppin Crow Bait. Backsteppin.

CROW: Counter meatface. Shuck it. The marks show clean through. Gauzy. Limpid to the bone. Look to the guard. That's where it hides. Lurkin like a wet hawk. Scuffle mark. Belt mark. Tune to the raw rumble. Tune chain. Chain. Chunk it meatface. Chunk this. Get off your ropeadope and chunk.

(REF *steps in and stops it.*)

REF: Hold it, hold it, hold it, hold it! Let's go to some neutral corners here. Both of you. Come on. Get to your corners.

HOSS: (*to* REF) What's the deal?

REF: Get to some neutral ground! I gotta reference this.

HOSS: Reference?

REF: Yeah, that's right. Reference. My books don't show this. I'm looking for jabs and hooks. Jab, jab, hook. Jab, jab, hook. That's the way I recognize it. I'm not seeing that.

HOSS: I didn't call you in here to analyze! Just score it!

CROW: Corn Belt Boogie!

HOSS: (*to* CROW) You stay outa this!

(BECKY *enters with* CHASER *and* DOC *close behind.*)

BECKY: Hoss! Hoss, we been clipped.

HOSS: What is this! I'm in a deadlock here! I can't even get off the mat.

CHASER: Eyes linked through the Net Web and got straight to the Keepers. Wanted to set this match up legit and they went thumbs down on him. Won't sanction it, won't even recognize it.

HOSS: What!

REF: (*leafing through reference book*) Here. Here's something here— (*reads*) "If a player shows any tendency toward unconsciousness, i.e., his tongue lolls out; his eyes roll; his breathing goes from bad to worse—"

HOSS: Somebody get this meatball outa here! I'm trying to fight a duel!

(DOC *goes to* REF *and gently persuades him to pack up his gear and leave.*)

HOSS: (*to* CHASER) What do you mean they won't sanction it? I'm in the top ten right? At least the top ten. I'm rising! I'm rising! They gotta give me a clean shot at this! It's automatic!

BECKY: He's a Gypsy, Hoss. Outside. They just won't ratify.

(CROW *starts doing a little hop and shuffle dance, singing softly to himself.*)

CROW: (*sings to himself*)

Doo dah, doo dah
Camptown race is five miles long
Doo dah, doo dah
Camptown ladies sing this song
All dee doo dah day

(CROW *continues in his own world as the rest of the dialogue goes on. He sings and dances demonically in the background.*)

CROW: (*continued*)

Gwaanah run all night
Gwannah run all day

Bet my money on dee bobtail nag
Somebody bet on dee bay

HOSS: (*simultaneous, over the top of* CROW) He's nothin! He's a freak! He's a corpse with clothes on! A haint! Look at him! How did he get in here!

BECKY: There's no point going head-to-head with him when it doesn't even count, Hoss.

HOSS: Count? Of course it counts! The Keepers are a joke! They've lost track of the real War. They're more outa touch than I am! I'm on the brink here, Becky. All I gotta do is knock this dog's dick in the dirt and I'm gone beyond. You understand? Beyond! I'm in a whole other domain. Suddenly, I'm King Cobra! Todo el Mundo!

BECKY: It won't happen, Hoss. They won't recognize it.

HOSS: *I'll* recognize it! Me! That's the skinny right there. *I'll* know. And that's all that counts. Now get this Cornhusker outa here. We're gonna go dry turkey until the drop.

CHASER: Hoss, look—there's no Ref, there's no score, there's no nothing. Empty wasteland.

HOSS: I'm goin down the road with this bonefreak and that's all there is to it. Head-to-head, til one's dead.

REF: (*to* DOC) The circuit's changed somewhat, from what I understand. Is that it? Is that what's happened here? I've been assigned to the wrong circuit?

DOC: That could well be it.

REF: This never could have happened in the days of the old chalkboard. You simply checked the chalk and jumped on the Greyhound.

DOC: The Greyhound. Yes. Have you collected all your items?

(DOC *helps* REF *gather his things and escorts him off.*)

REF: I was a Union man. Things were organized.

DOC: (*helping* REF) It's unfortunate, yes. We all seem to get swept along in the tidal wave. I was a Vaquero, myself.

REF: A what?

DOC: It doesn't matter. Have you got all your things?

REF: I'm being shipped out. Is that it? Discarded?

DOC: It's just that—well, everything has slipped way beyond the rules.

REF: The rules haven't slipped. That's one thing for sure. Rules are rules. Can't change that.

DOC: No, I suppose not.

HOSS: Get him outa here!

REF: (*as* DOC *escorts him offstage*) A game's a game. Rules make the game. Take the rules away and what have you got? Bibbidy bobbidy boop. Answer me that. A lotta pissin in the wind. That's what you got. Pissin in the wind. They better have my check waitin for me back in Lincoln, that's all I can say.

(DOC *and* REF *have gone, leaving* HOSS, CROW, CHASER, *and* BECKY. CROW *cools down off his mad dance and begins to slowly circle* HOSS. BECKY *and* CHASER *move back.*)

CHASER: Hoss, look, there's no savvy to this. No Gold. You could wind up whiplashed and counterfeit.

HOSS: (*to* CHASER) Step back, Shotgun. There's another deal been dealt here.

CROW: Here's a posy! Here's a posy! Judges? Rules? Law-breaker. Set yer sick entourage up. Bring 'em on in here, thick. Line 'em up. They rule it. Fair is fair. They scam it. I'm game. Ready for the outcome.

HOSS: (*to* CROW) Wing it, dogmeat.

CROW: Eeeew! Freejump jigee! Step right off in the crystal blue. There he's sailin! Look there! Now! That's him!

(DOC *reenters and joins* BECKY *and* CHASER *on the sidelines as they watch* CROW *stalk* HOSS *in the middle.*)

CROW: (*to* DOC *as he sees him enter*) Join 'em up, join 'em up, join 'em up. We be circling the wagons here. We be old-time schooling. We be hip-hopping, rag-moppin, doo-wop diddle boppin. How many lines we gotta cross before you all git the big picture? HUH! How many corny lines we gotta bust yer silly chops with before the dawn cracks yer ass wide open! HUH! You cipher me as some crude anomaly? Is that it? I'm the Norm, Jim. I am the fuckin river! And I've gone clean up over the banks. Now, you swim! Lemme see y'all pump them bony elbows and blow snot. (*to* DOC) Come on, Viejo! Pump it!

HOSS: Missed the whole era. Never touched the backseat.

(CROW *charges* HOSS *savagely, setting him off balance. He gets right after him, relentless in his assault.*)

CROW: That's it! That's it! Back! Way back! We wanna go back. We wanna go way back, dark. We wanna git a hole so deep the feet and tongue go lost. Down back coughin in the corner. Dyin from the wet lung. Back down lonely in the dayroom. Dyin for the Daddy. Dyin for the Mama. Dyin for the agelong Frankenstein Fambily. Dyin for the Kin Folk, misery and sin. Dim down. Dim down. Back. Go way back yonder. Desperate honor. Glory for the Black Man. Glory for the brother. The Gray Blue Black Catastrophe. And then get horny. Now git yer horns up. Get drippin red now. Here he comes stormin! Here he comes knockin over pay phones. He be rippin now! Jacked way up on his own dead juices. Rollin over Beethoven, Rockin pneumonia. Befloppin to the Fat Man. Drivin to the small talk. Here he comes. Drive by. Gotta make his big mark. Take a shot at the carhop. Now there's a deed. Full of honor. Full of greed. Now we find him in the can-can. Bewildered. Stunned. Doin time, time. Whinin like a wino. Whinin in the dim dim. Whinin all the time oh. Whinin, whinin.

(CROW *slides off and away from* HOSS, *leaving him shaken, reeling.*)

BECKY: Hoss! Just give him the crib. Let's slide outa here. He's too fast.

DOC: I didn't even see half that shit comin, Hoss.

HOSS: He's fast. He's flash.

CROW: (*more distance from* HOSS, *quieter*) In the slammer he's a useless. But he does his schoolin. Tries to keep a blind face. Storin up his hate cells. Drip by drip. Thinks he's got it comin. Bangin out the street signs. Makin do his time time. Transforms into a Candy Cock to get his reprieve shine. Shinin through the dark time. Lost in the long sleeve. Long lost. Long ache in the blue moon wake. Just staked like Jesus to his bare rope bed. Shakin in the moonshine. Shakin. Calls it bitter bloody medicine and feels his whole sad man go under. Boom. Like that.

CHASER: Hoss. I ain't stayin for this.

HOSS: (*to* CHASER) You stay! You stand right here! You be a witness. I'm gonna turn him over.

CROW: Over, under, around, and through. The badder the boy, the deeper the blue. The string fright. The raw face. Bone fear. White. Dread brings him out in macho shoes and strings him up, dick hard. Dead. Dread. It's dread. Right? Dead to the core and dressed slick for the afterlife. It's all over Rover. Roll over. Bark twice and die. Bark now! Book it. Whimper one time for the life of crime.

HOSS: (*deep Delta Blues voice*) Yeah, well I hear about all that kinda 'lectric machine gun music. Bazooka drool. Brains drippin off the ceiling. All that kinda 'lectric shuffle. Chi-town. North.

CROW: Hoodee, hoodee! Who we got here? Satchemup Joe? Satchemo?

HOSS: I hear you boys hook up in the toilet and play to the mirror all through the night. Imaging. Imaging. Scarfin chords off the radio. Thievin lead lines. Imitation harmonies.

CROW: Yubah. Twelve bars does goes a long way.

HOSS: It come down a long way. It come down by every damn black backstreet you can move sideways through. Deep Ellum. Maybelline. Before that. Long before. Snaking through giant dripping rubber trees. Cypress grove. Cheetahs shakin to it. Cipher, dead bird?

CROW: Hidee, hidee! We be trackin now! We be on the whiff.

HOSS: Fast tongue. Fast fingers. Speed. So fast everything blew out yer back window and you never even turned to look. Never saw it streaming, stuck to cactus like dead flags off Highway 66. Something lost now, boy? Something lost to you? Something way bygone.

CROW: Chub up. Chub it up.

HOSS: You miss the origins, milkface. Little Brother with the keyboard on his back. Hunched through the Turpentine

Circuit. Mule driven. Piano strapped to his buckboard. Jimmy Yancey. Big Maceo. Meade Lux. Back then you get hung you couldn't play the blues. You get strung from limb to limbo. They'd sic the Hellhounds on yer trail. Back when the boogie wasn't named and every cathouse had its Professor. Hookers grindin to the ivory tinkle. Diplomats and sailors gettin laid side by side to the blues. Gettin laid so bad the United States Navy had to close down Storyville. Then the move began. North. Chi-town. King Oliver. Ma Rainey. Blind Lemon. They all come and got the gangsters hoppin.

CROW: He's gone bygone tootie again. Long gone. Sacriligo! Drifted back to smoke and stink. The Past never happened! The past never did! Yonder yore. It's air and nothing more. Air! Hallucination. Empty, empty. Sorrow and cremation!

HOSS: You a blind minstrel with a phony shuffle, Jim. You got a wide wound gaping 'tween the chords and the pickin. Chuck Berry and all his ghosts can't even mend you up. You doin a pantomime in the eye of the hurricane and ain't even got the sense to signal for help.

CROW: Help, oh help, oh help me doctor! I'm about to testify! Mercy, mercy, I'm a gonna die.

HOSS: You lost the barrelhouse, you lost the honky-tonk. You lost yer feelings in a suburban country club the first time they asked you to play "Rising River Blues" for the Debutante Ball.

CROW: You forgit that I'm from nowhere. Horsehair. I was never raised up. I have simply arisen. Epiphany!

HOSS: You ripped your own self off and now all you got is yer poison to call yer gift. Yer a punk chump with a sequin noseband and you'll need more than a Les Paul Gibson to bring you home.

CROW: Home! Home? Home is where the heart is! That's easy ditty. I got no heart to tie me down. I'm everywhere at once. Ubiquitous! Omnipotent! I'll tap dance right across your sentimental rainy street every time you put your big toe in. I'll shake yer booty while you weep for the naked ancestors. I'll eat your maudlin lunch while you pay tribute to drivel and fantasy stick. I'm burnin from the inside out, Mighty Man. I got no time for retrospect. I'm in the charred zone. Gone. Blasted in oblivion. For me, this match is done dick. Dead. All you been doin is spinnin yer wheels from bell one.

(CROW *makes a move as though to leave.*)

HOSS: Wait! You can't walk outa here! This match ain't over!

DOC: Let him go, Hoss.

HOSS: Nothing's been decided!

CROW: (*turns to* HOSS) Oh, you want finality?

HOSS: I want—I want—some kinda satisfaction. Are you conceding? Is that it? Giving up the ghost?

CROW: I was jest gonna go git me a cheeseburger.

HOSS: Look—Look—This can't be the—We're in a fight to the death here, aren't we? High stakes. This is supposed to be—

CROW: This is nothin. This is jack.

HOSS: You can't just dismiss this! I'm a King Marker! One of the best! You took me on for a reason.

CROW: I was jest curious how the other half lived.

HOSS: You challenged *me*!

CHASER: There's no challenge without the Keepers' sanction, Hoss.

HOSS: Fuck the Keepers! He's in my house! He's right here in front of me.

CROW: Are you sure? Are you dead certain on that score? Are you sure I'm not just some faintly figment? Here— You got a shiv. Cut my wrist. See if blood comes. Do it!

(CROW *holds out his wrist, offering it to* HOSS. *Pause.*)

CROW: Surest sign of humankind. Right? Blood? Sangre. Red human pool.

BECKY: Hoss, don't. Don't even think about it. He's past some Warlock mode.

CROW: (*holding out his wrist to* HOSS) She's got that cocked. Out beyond. Mas alla. Where thought drops off into rippling sheets of shiny black. Where thought can't come near to touching. Do it! Cut this thin band and see what pours forth. Might be yer biggest nightmare yet to come.

(HOSS *pulls out his knife and approaches* CROW.)

DOC: Hoss, there's the Devil in this. Bonefaced Devil. Don't step in.

CROW: (*arm still out*) Oh, sin again! Oh sin! Fear and pity. Nitty gritty. Better listen up to your Viejo medicine man. He been around the auditorium two or three times.

87

(HOSS *pauses.*)

CHASER: We can call it a draw, Hoss. Just mark it down to a photo and let him waltz. There's Phoenix up ahead. Mojo Root Force. We can pump the road again.

HOSS: (*with knife*) I'll know the bottom of this. Whatever comes. I'll know it sure.

CROW: That's my puppy. Seek the truth. Seek the truth. Your Americano groove. Rip and shred it. Wring it dry with both hands held way high and scream now to your grand Manifesto. Your Supreme Divine Providenso. Look your monster in the eye and scream now. Testify!

HOSS: (*approaching* CROW *with knife*) I just might skin you. I just might. But there's a fascination. Why is that? Some—premonition. Meera. Some cutting edge where this thing might flip. Some mangy mad dog fear this blade might turn itself around and slip.

CROW: There, the light comes crying through! There, the bright tiny sliver! Peel that eyeball back a taste.

HOSS: Why this envy? This covet for the opposite?

CROW: You recognize me now?

HOSS: I almost wish—

CROW: Wishing, wishing, ring the bell. Toss yer copper tinkle. Go straight to Hell.

HOSS: No! There's something—There's something too familiar. Like I just missed it. A shadow roll. A dance partner. Face-to-face. What is this I'm seeing! Me in you!

CROW: A blasted crack! Hold steady now. Mind the mind. This may be your one and only shining time.

DOC: Hoss, he's working something on you. I've seen this. Brujo jive.

HOSS: I could be you. An inch or two and I'd be sitting in yer skin. This match could flip around.

CROW: Oh, so now you wanna swap? Do the rage re-bop. Break yer cage and fly to my dark street. Luz. Luz en la noche del cuerpo!

HOSS: Show me! Show me! Just an inch and I could straddle. I'm a one and only man. A genuine original! I could make this leap. Just reach an inch. Just reach!

CROW: A miracle mile wouldn't cut it.

HOSS: No, no, no! Help me to it!

BECKY: Hoss! You've crossed soft. You're going Roadkill now.

CROW: So you wanna be a rocker. Study the moves. Jerry Lee Lewis. Cop some blue suede shoes. Switch yer head like Carl Perkins. Put yer ass in a grind. Talkin sock it to it, get the image in line. Get the image in line, boy. The fantasy whine. It's all over dee street and you caint buy dee time. Caint buy dee beebop. Caint buy dee slide. Got dee fantasy blues and no place to hide.

HOSS: Not that! Not that! Not back! Show me! I need to see it. Show me the skull! Crack me through!

CROW: Bone and marrow, bone and marrow. Scarf that! Yer scammin an empty body, boo. Plow and harrow!

HOSS: How could this happen? This ain't the way it's supposed to be! Look at me! Everything was topped off. I had fingertip control. Push-button. Flush. Now I'm quaking like some sudden whirlpool's at my feet. Show me! Show me something! Where's the man in me! Show me that at least.

CROW: Man's too tough, Leathers. Shoulda shucked that one long ago.

HOSS: What's left then?

CROW: Hoodoo Haint. The techno-fantasy bop. Start there and then skid. Image menu. Dial it up.

HOSS: How? Start where? Where do I stand! Where the fuck do I stand now!

CROW: Solo, Leathers. Simple solo. Cut away in oblivion.

HOSS: You've got to let me into this.

CROW: Nada, nada. Upside down. Inside out. You made *me,* beyond a doubt. I'm *your* sliced creation. Your whole damn nation. You built me slowly, block by block. From TV tube to hip-hop rock. You dripped me dry-boned, bloodless, headless for your pleasure. Now, you wanna call me "mastah"? You wanna slave to me now, showboat bastard? Chuck it. Cut it to the wrist! Let gush this mind-raped vision of your gift.

HOSS: I'm seeing something. Something in there. Just a whisper.

CROW: (*whisper*) Choog it. Choog it. Catch ahold.

HOSS: Here! It's right here. Close. Coming at me. Mean and tough and cool. Untouchable. Here he is. You see?

CROW: Catch him fast.

DOC: He's lost it now.

HOSS: (*points to* CROW's *chest*) No, look! Right here it comes! Emergence. I see him now. A true killer. True to his heart. True to his voice. Whole. Unshakable. There! See? He's coming out! Right toward me now. There! Stepping out! A body as sure as you or me. See? Identity!

CROW: Snatch him up now. Take ahold.

(CHASER *makes a move toward* HOSS. DOC *stops him.*)

DOC: No! Don't bump him. Let this ghost roll past him.

HOSS: (*seeing phantom image*) His cold eyes. His cut. Look! He knows his fate. Beyond doubt. Here he is. True courage in every move. Old, old, ancient hero. Plunged headlong through fear and come out clean. Wears his scars in humility. Died a million deaths. Tortured and pampered. Holds no grudge. No blame. No guilt. Passed beyond sorrow and tears. Beyond ache for the world. Pitiless. Indifferent. And riding a state of grace. It ain't me. It ain't me! It ain't me! See?

(HOSS *slashes out with knife at phantom image; whirls around to face it again behind him.*)

HOSS: You see it scream? You hear its hollow face? Its agony. Its scar's broke open now. See? I've slashed him clean. Here! Here in his dark throat.

(*He slashes out again and whirls.*)

HOSS: Here! Here in his broken knees! His baggy sleeves cut to ribbons! Cut! Slashed! Mutilated from my dreams!

(*He keeps cutting, slashing, and whirling at phantom.*)

HOSS: Shredded! See! See him stagger helpless! See him stunned and hopeless! Ghost face. Ghastly partner. Now! Now you're doomed. Now!

(HOSS *turns the knife on himself and stabs his belly.*)

HOSS: No way back in. No reentry. Gone! Gone from me. Long gone from me.

(*He collapses to the floor, face down on the knife. A river of bright red blood begins to pour from him and continues through the end of the play.*)

CROW: Perfect, Leathers. Absoloo. A genius mark. Took yer sweet time sliding home but finally found the killing zone.

(BECKY *moves slowly to* HOSS*'s crumpled body and kneels beside him.*)

BECKY: (*to* CROW *as she moves*) You played him for this. You had him fixed.

CROW: From the drop, sweets. From the drop. A fishtail always gives itself away by the wake it makes.

DOC: Same with a snake. I've seen that. Sidewinders. Diamondbacks. Little reminders which side of the crick to strike your camp.

CROW: Yeah, you been out there, Viejo man. You be out there again now. Pack your sack.

CHASER: (*approaching* HOSS*'s body*) He was knockin at the door. He was right up there with the best of 'em. He came the long route, though. Not like you. He earned his nook. He was a Marker. A true Marker.

CROW: He was backed up by his own suction, son. Didn't answer to no name but loser. All that power goin backwards. Creates a helluva vortex. It's good he shut the oven. Fact, I did him a favor. He was stopping up force fields from here to Salt Lake City. Lookit all the air I've opened up for us. All the blazing road.

CHASER: Us? I'm not packin with you, chump.

CROW: Honor and loyalty. Remnants of the Royalty. Dirty, cryin shame how they've vanished with the game.

(CROW *sings as lights dim slowly to black.* HOSS*'s blood continues to flow toward the audience.*)

CROW: *Song:* "Sweet Lullaby"

SWEET LULLABY

Time is quit
Look it in the eye
In blood we sit
In dark we die
Don't blink now
Sweet lullaby

Clock is stopped
Stare into the skull
Into the face
Invisible
Hold me close
Sweet actual

   Come and drape across my knee
   Rain through my street
   Come and blow this candle out
   Incomplete

Sam Shepard

Time is quit
Look it in the eye
In blood we sit
In dark we die
Fare the well
Sweet lullaby

Time is quit
Look it in the eye
In blood we sit
In dark we die
Don't blink now
Sweet lullaby

BURIED CHILD

A Play

In this newly revised edition of the Pulitzer Prize–winning play *Buried Child*, a scene of madness greets Vince and his girlfriend when they arrive at the farmhouse of his hard-drinking grandparents, who seem to have no idea who he is. Nor does his father, Tilden, a hulking former All-American football player, or his uncle who has lost one of his legs to a chain saw. Only the memory of an unwanted child, buried in an undisclosed location, can hope to deliver this family from its sin.

Drama/0-307-27497-7

CRUISING PARADISE

Tales

A boy travels to a roadside inn to retrieve the mattress on which his drunken father burned to death. A mortified actor bulldozes his way through the Mexican border bureaucracy by pretending to be Spencer Tracy. A man and a woman quarrel desperately in a South Dakota motel room and part company for reasons neither can understand. The stories in *Cruising Paradise* map the places where our culture is defined, from a writer who has become synonymous with the recklessness, stoicism, and solitude of American manhood.

Fiction/Short Stories/0-679-74217-4

THE GOD OF HELL

A Play

Frank and Emma are a quiet, respectable couple who raise cows on their Wisconsin farm. Soon after they agree to put up Frank's old friend Haynes, who is on the lam from a secret government project involving plutonium, they're visited by Welch, an unctuous government bureaucrat from hell. His aggressive patriotism puts Frank, Emma, and Haynes on the defensive, transforming a heartland American household into a scene of torture and promoting a radioactive brand of conformity with a dangerously long half-life.

Drama/1-4000-9651-0

GREAT DREAM OF HEAVEN
Stories

A woman driving her mother's ashes across the country has a strangely transcendent run-in with an injured hawk. Two aging widowers, in Stetsons and bolo ties, together make a daily pilgrimage to the local Denny's, only to be divided by the attentions of their favorite waitress. A boy watches a "remedy man" tame a wild stallion, a contest that mirrors his own struggle with his father. Peering unblinkingly into the chasms that separate fathers and sons, husbands and wives, friends and strangers, these lyrical tales bear the unmistakable signature of an American master.

Fiction/Short Stories/0-375-70452-3

SIMPATICO
A Play

Carter ought to be managing his thoroughbred business in Kentucky. Instead, he is in a room in Cucamonga, Nowheresville, U.S.A., trying to get back in the good graces of Vinnie, the one man who has the power to destroy him. From the beginning, Sam Shepard's *Simpatico* launches us into the world of horse racing, where high society meets the low life and the line between winners and losers is as treacherously thin as a razor blade.

Drama/0-679-76317-1

THE LATE HENRY MOSS, EYES FOR CONSUELA, WHEN THE WORLD WAS GREEN
Three Plays

In *The Late Henry Moss*, two estranged brothers confront the past as they piece together the drunken fishing expedition that preceded their father's death. In *Eyes for Consuela*, a vacationing American encounters a knife-toting Mexican bandit on a gruesome quest. And in *When the World Was Green*, a journalist in search of her father interviews an old man who resolved a vendetta by murdering the wrong man.

Drama/1-4000-3079-X

STATES OF SHOCK, FAR NORTH, SILENT TONGUE
A Play and Two Screenplays

Sam Shepard's writing tears through the envelope between prose and poetry and between pop culture and myth. In the play *States of Shock*, a nostalgic colonel and his mutilated guest celebrate a bizarre anniversary—and in the process reopen the wounds of war, sexuality, and familial betrayal. The screenplay *Far North* looks fondly and sadly across the gap of gender and generation. And in his screenplay *Silent Tongue*, Shepard turns the history of the white presence on the frontier into something resembling Greek tragedy.

Drama/0-679-74218-2

THE UNSEEN HAND
And Other Plays

If you visit Sam Shepard country, expect to find bayous, deserts, and junkyards where dreams rust alongside abandoned Chevys. Prepare to meet broken gunmen, refugees from distant galaxies, slavering swamp things, and California highway patrolmen. Sam Shepard does nothing less than renew America's myths—and sometimes he invents them from scratch. In these fourteen works for the theater, our most audacious living playwright sets genres and archetypes spinning, with utterly mesmerizing results.

Drama/0-679-76789-4

VINTAGE BOOKS
Available at your local bookstore, or call toll-free to order:
1-800-793-2665 (credit cards only).